THOMAS CRANE PUBLIC LIBRARY
QUINCY MASS
CITY APPROPRIATION

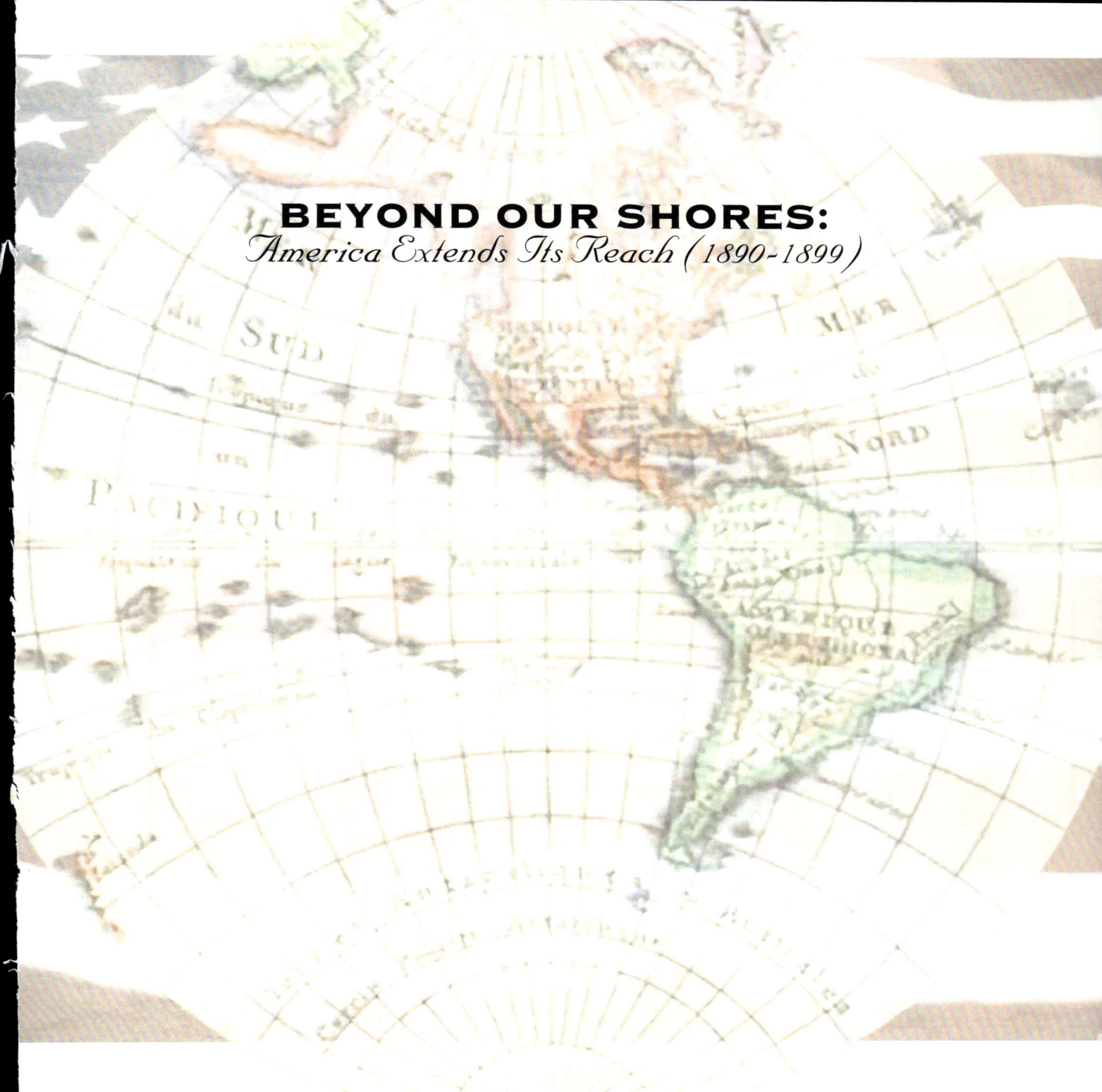

BEYOND OUR SHORES:
America Extends Its Reach (1890-1899)

HOW AMERICA BECAME AMERICA

TITLE LIST

THE NORTHERN COLONIES: FREEDOM TO WORSHIP (1600-1770)

THE SOUTHERN COLONIES: THE SEARCH FOR WEALTH (1600-1770)

AMERICA IS BORN (1770-1800)

THOMAS JEFFERSON AND THE GROWING UNITED STATES (1800-1811)

WARS AT HOME: AMERICA FORMS AN IDENTITY (1812-1820)

REMEMBER THE ALAMO: AMERICANS FIGHT FOR TEXAS (1820-1845)

AMERICANS MOVE WEST (1846-1860)

THE CIVIL WAR: AMERICA TORN APART (1860-1865)

AMERICAN WILDERNESS: ALASKA AND THE NATIONAL PARKS (1865-1890)

BEYOND OUR SHORES: AMERICA EXTENDS ITS REACH (1890-1899)

A SHIFTING ROLE: AMERICA AND THE WORLD (1900-1912)

AMERICA IN THE 20TH CENTURY (1913-1999)

CONNECTING THE 21ST CENTURY TO THE PAST: WHAT MAKES AMERICA AMERICA? (2000-THE PRESENT)

HOW AMERICA BECAME AMERICA

BEYOND OUR SHORES:
America Extends Its Reach (1890-1899)

By Constance Sharp

Mason Crest

BEYOND OUR SHORES: AMERICA EXTENDS ITS REACH

Mason Crest
370 Reed Road
Broomall, Pennsylvania 19008
www.masoncrest.com

Copyright © 2013 by Mason Crest, an imprint of National Highlights, Inc. All rights reserved. No part of this publication may be reproduced or transmitted in any form or by any means, electronic or mechanical, including photocopying, recording, taping, or any information storage and retrieval system, without permission from the publisher.

Printed and bound in Hashemite Kingdom of Jordan.

First printing
9 8 7 6 5 4 3 2 1

Library of Congress Cataloging-in-Publication Data

Sharp, Constance.
 Beyond our shores : America extends its reach,1890-1899 / Constance Sharp.
    p. cm. — (How America became America)
 Includes index.
 ISBN 978-1-4222-2406-9 (hardcover) — ISBN 978-1-4222-2396-3 (hardcover series) — ISBN 978-1-4222-9316-4 (ebook)
 1. United States—Territorial expansion—History—19th century—Juvenile literature. 2. United States—Foreign relations—1865-1898—Juvenile literature. I. Title.
 E713.S525 2013
 973.8—dc23
                                         2012010665

Produced by Harding House Publishing Services, Inc.
www.hardinghousepages.com
Cover design by Torque Advertising + Design.

CONTENTS

Time Line   6
1. America Grows Up   9
2. Hawaii   17
3. Cuba   27
4. Puerto Rico   37
Find Out More   44
Index   46
About the Author   47
About the Consultant   48

BEYOND OUR SHORES: AMERICA EXTENDS ITS REACH

- 1493–Christopher Columbus discovers Puerto Rico.
- 1511–Hatuey flees the island of Hispañola for Cuba.
- 1519–Ferdinand Magellan arrives in the Philippines.
- 1778–James Cook lands on the island of Kuai'I; he is killed by island natives in 1779.
- 1795–Chief Kamehameha I unites the Hawaiian Islands.
- 1802–The first sugar mill is opened on the Hawaiian Islands.
- 1823–President James Monroe writes the Monroe Doctrine.

Time Line

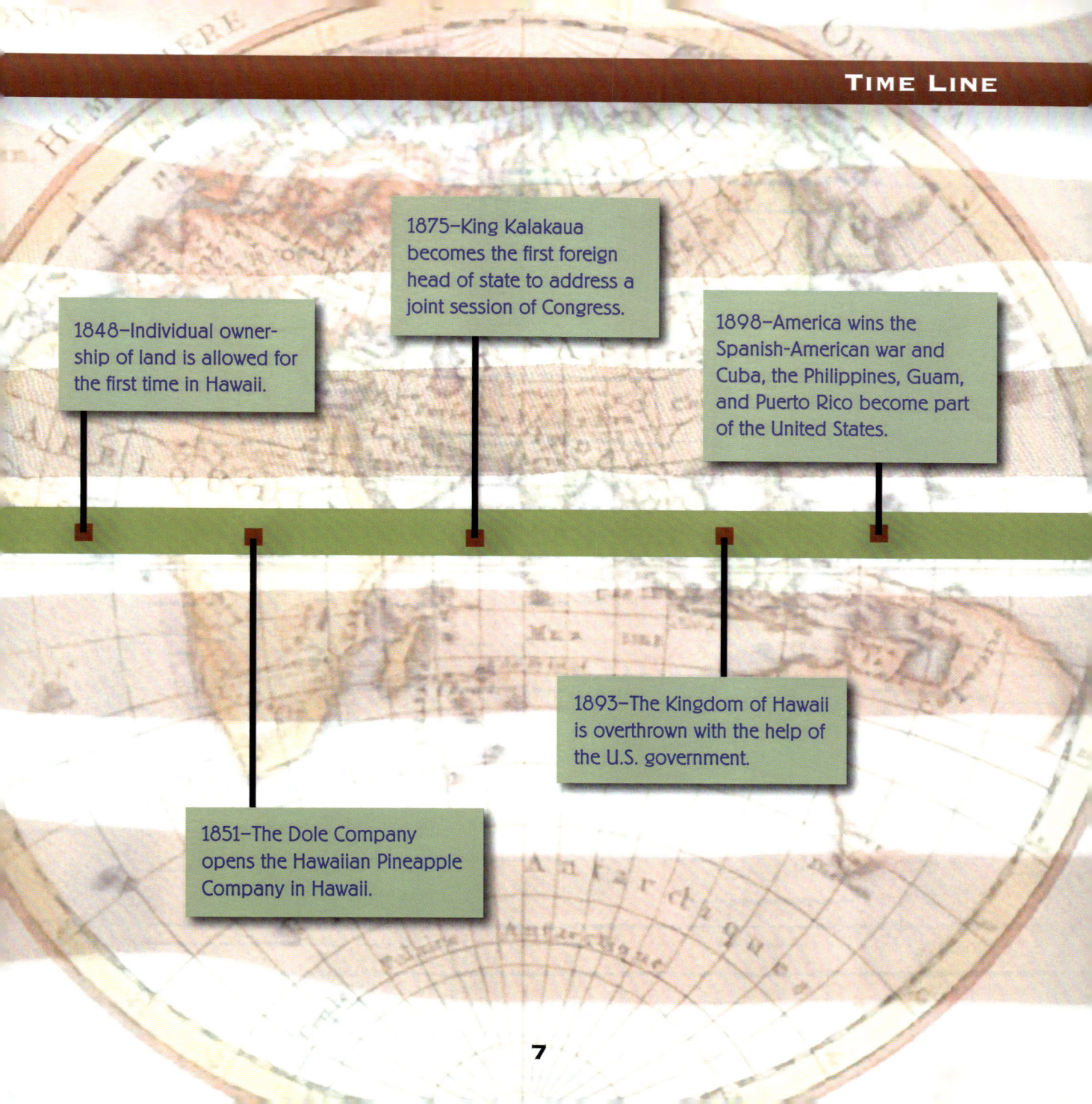

1848 – Individual ownership of land is allowed for the first time in Hawaii.

1851 – The Dole Company opens the Hawaiian Pineapple Company in Hawaii.

1875 – King Kalakaua becomes the first foreign head of state to address a joint session of Congress.

1893 – The Kingdom of Hawaii is overthrown with the help of the U.S. government.

1898 – America wins the Spanish-American war and Cuba, the Philippines, Guam, and Puerto Rico become part of the United States.

Chapter One
AMERICA GROWS UP

Sooner or later most children rebel against their parents. They want to stand on their own two feet. They no longer want to do everything their parents tell them to do. That's just part of growing up. And the young country of America felt the same way. America wanted to break away from her mother country, Britain.

Of course, the first time America rebelled was back in the 1700s. Americans fought the Revolutionary War so their country could be free from Britain. But that was just the beginning. In some ways, America stayed close to Britain. After all, the two countries were a lot alike. Many Americans came from Britain. They still had friends and family in Britain. In many ways, Americans and the British still thought the same way. They had the same values. Many of the same things were important to them.

But in other ways, Britain and America were very different. Sometimes America wanted one thing, while Britain wanted something else. Just like in any family, they had arguments. They bumped heads.

And at the same time, both countries were changing. They were both getting bigger. America was no longer a baby nation. And England had turned into an **empire**. "The

---

An **empire** is when a government has control over lands that are separate from it. These lands were once free and separate countries.

BEYOND OUR SHORES: AMERICA EXTENDS ITS REACH

sun never sets on the English Empire," was a common saying in those days. That meant that the English Empire stretched all the way around the globe. At any hour, somewhere, the sun was shining on British land.

As children grow up, they often imitate their parents. That's what the United States did. By the end of the nineteenth century, America was trying to break away further from Britain. At the same time, America was trying to be more like Britain. Americans were thinking about building their own empire.

THE MONROE DOCTRINE

Back in 1832, President James Monroe made an important statement. His statement is called the Monroe Doctrine. That statement would shape the way America thought of itself all the way up to the twenty-first century.

The Monroe Doctrine said that Europe could no longer build colonies in North America or South America. Then it went one step further. It said that it was the United States' job to protect North and South America from other countries. This meant America had the right to get mixed up in any war that took place in North or South America. This happened in 1895.

VENEZUELA

Great Britain had a colony in Guiana, on the northern coast of South America. The land lay along the border of Venezuela. Venezuelans said that Britain had claimed several hundred miles of their land. Venezuela wanted the countries of the world to help them settle the question. Britain refused to even talk about it. The two countries had been angry with each other for years.

Grover Cleveland became President of the United States in 1892. He was worried that Britain might claim even more land in South America. He didn't want that to happen.

AMERICA GROWS UP

Map of Venezuela.

BEYOND OUR SHORES: America Extends Its Reach

EMPIRES IN HISTORY

One of the earliest and most powerful empires was the Roman Empire. It once spread across most of Europe. Centuries later, the great European countries—Spain, England, and France—built their own empires. They built colonies on the "new land" they discovered on the other side of the Atlantic Ocean. Slowly, Spain and France became less powerful. England (or Britain) grew in strength. Now, England no longer has an empire. Some people say America is trying to build something like an empire of its own by controlling what happens in much of the world.

Empires can be good for countries in some ways. The stronger country can bring schools, better roads, and better health care. In other ways, though, they can be bad. They take away the other countries' freedom.

What do you think? Are empires good or bad?

He didn't want Great Britain to become any stronger than it was already. So he wrote a letter to Great Britain.

The British were angry. They said that the Monroe Doctrine was just something Americans had made up. The British didn't think it was a real law.

Now President Cleveland was angry. He didn't want a war. But he didn't want to back down either.

The British didn't want a war either. Eventually, they agreed to let an **international tribunal** settle their argument with Venezuela. The tribunal came up with a compromise. Great Britain would get to keep the land it had already claimed. It could not claim any more land, though.

Nothing much happened really. But it was important because this was the first time American had acted on the Monroe Doctrine. It was the first time the United States insisted it had the right to get mixed up in something that had nothing to do with America.

HISTORY'S STORIES

History is full of stories. The people who take part in events all have their own stories. Those stories depend on their point of view. For example, think about the stories the American settlers told. Those stories had to do with courage and freedom. Then think of the stories the **Native** people told who lost their lands to those settlers. Their stories would have been very different! Both sets of stories have their own truth.

An **international tribunal** is a court that settles problems between countries.

Native is a word for the people who lived in North and South America before white people came there.

BEYOND OUR SHORES: AMERICA EXTENDS ITS REACH

Symbolic representation of England's growing empire.

America Grows Up

Stories are also powerful. They help shape the future. They push people to act in certain ways. The Monroe Doctrine was one of those powerful stories.

The Monroe Doctrine would lead the United States into war. It would play a big role in many of Americans' stories for years to come. Those stories would end up touching the lives of countless people who lived in other lands. One of those lands was the peaceful island nation of Hawaii.

President James Monroe

According to mythology, the Hawaiian Islands are the children of the earth and sky.

Chapter Two
HAWAII

Long before America came to Hawaii, the people who lived there had their own stories. The Hawaiians said that Papa, the Earth-Mother, and Wakea, the Sky-Father, had given birth to the islands of Hawaii and Maui. Their grandchild was the taro plant. Everything was linked together. The world was alive. It breathed. It was like a person. It grew. It was good.

Stories like these were passed down from parents to children for hundreds of years. They had been brought to Hawaii hundreds of years ago by Polynesian settlers. These people explored the entire Pacific Ocean. They settled on the islands.

THE ANCIENT LAND OF HAWAII

Centuries before Europeans ever dared to sail out into the Atlantic Ocean, the ancient Hawaiians were sailing all over the Pacific. They understood the natural world in ways that Europeans didn't. This made them good sailors.

Taro is a plant that has starchy, good-to-eat roots, a little like potatoes.

BEYOND OUR SHORES: AMERICA EXTENDS ITS REACH

At home, they were also good farmers. They grew more than 200 kinds of sweet potatoes and taro. They used **irrigation** to water their fields. Their farming was so good that they didn't have to work very hard to feed lots of people.

Most ancient Hawaiians only worked about four hours a day. But they built the largest temples in all the Pacific. They also built the fastest canoes. They created beautiful dances and poetry. They made cloth out of bark.

POLYNESIA

In the South Pacific Ocean there is a group of more than 1,000 small islands. These are known as Polynesia. The Native people who live in these islands share many of same customs and beliefs. They speak the same language. For hundreds of years, they have been skilled sailors who used the stars for direction.

These people weren't perfect. They could be mean to each other. But most of the time, they lived in peace. They saw God everywhere. They prayed about everything. They had rules that told them how to get along with each other. They shared the land where they lived. They shared the work. They shared their food. And they hardly ever got sick. They'd never even had a cold!

Irrigation is a way to bring water to farmland using pipes.

Hawaii

Ancient Hawaiians

BEYOND OUR SHORES: AMERICA EXTENDS ITS REACH

Hawaii contains many different ecosystems.

EUROPEANS ARRIVE IN HAWAII

In 1778, everything changed in Hawaii. A British explorer named Captain James Cook landed on one of the Hawaiian islands. Now the rest of the world would find out about Hawaii. Their peaceful, ancient way of living would come to an end.

In the years to come, American and British ships often stopped at the Hawaiian Islands. The ships would stock up there on food and fresh water. The sailors told other people about how beautiful the islands were. Other white people started coming to the islands.

They brought change with them. They didn't follow the laws Hawaiians had followed for centuries. The Hawaiians saw that nothing happened to the white people who broke the laws. Soon some Hawaiians no longer followed the ancient laws either. This meant that their whole way of life would begin to change.

The white people also brought germs with them. The people who lived on the islands had no **immunity** against these germs. Thousands and thousands of Hawaiians got sick and died.

Missionaries also came to Hawaii. They taught Christianity to the Hawaiians. But they also taught the Hawaiians about other things. White people didn't understand the islanders' religion. The Hawaiians' way of living made no sense to them. They thought they were helping the Hawaiians by teaching them new ways of doing things

Hawaiians had never used money. They didn't own land. Instead, they shared everything. Now, though, they learned about money. They learned about being rich. They learned to own land. Instead of growing crops to share with each other, now they learned

---

Immunity is the ability to fight off germs and not get sick.

BEYOND OUR SHORES: AMERICA EXTENDS ITS REACH

to sell their crops for money. Instead, of growing food for themselves, they started growing sugarcane to sell.

In the 70 years after Captain Cook arrived in Hawaii, everything changed. Before long, the Monroe Doctrine would also reach Hawaii. And then everything would change even more.

PINEAPPLE AND THE MONROE DOCTRINE

Have you ever eaten Dole pineapple? You probably have. But you probably didn't know how important Dole was to the history of Hawaii.

In 1851, James Drummond Dole started the Hawaiian Pineapple Company. The company planted and grew pineapples.

Hawaiian pineapple pickers

Then it picked the pineapples and put them in cans. It shipped the pineapples to America. For the first time, Americans could buy pineapple in almost any grocery store.

Mr. Dole was an honest businessman. He didn't understand that his business was helping to change Hawaiians' lives.

Hawaii

And while Mr. Dole was building his business, people from Britain were also building businesses in Hawaii. Great Britain hoped that Hawaii would become part of the British Empire. The United States didn't want that to happen. The Americans who lived in Hawaii—like Mr. Dole—didn't want it to happen either. Using the Monroe Doctrine again, American told Great Britain to back off.

The Americans who lived in Hawaii were less than 20 percent of the whole population. But they controlled more than 80 percent of Hawaii's wealth. This made them very powerful. They decided to form their own government.

In 1893, they took Hawaii away from its queen. Sanford B. Dole, who now owned the Hawaiian Pineapple Company, became the president of the new government. The new government wrote new laws. Now only people who owned large pieces of land could vote. People who could not read, write, or speak English could not be **citizens**. This left out most of the native Hawaiians.

The new government wanted to become part of the United States. The white landowners knew this was the best way to protect their land and businesses from the British.

Meanwhile, America was in the midst of a war with Spain over other islands in the Pacific Ocean. Hawaii was a good stopping place for warships headed to those islands. The United States realized that having a naval base at Hawaii could be a good idea. Americans didn't want Spain to attack Hawaii.

Citizens are the people in a country whose rights are protected by law.

BEYOND OUR SHORES: AMERICA EXTENDS ITS REACH

Princess Kaiulani

A SAD DAY FOR HAWAII

The Hawaiian government had a big ceremony and party on the day when Hawaii became a part of the United States. But the woman who had been queen, Queen Liliuokalani, and her daughter, Princess Kaiulani, did not go to the party. Many native Hawaiians gathered at the Queen's home. For them, it was the saddest day they had ever known.

Today, many people in Hawaii still feel that Hawaii should be a separate free country. They want to give Hawaii back to native Hawaiians. In 1993, the U.S. government did apologize to native Hawaiians for overthrowing their kingdom. For some Hawaiians, this apology is too little too late.

In 1898, the Hawaiian Islands became part of the United States. President Dole now became the governor of the new territory. His government continued to rule the islands for several years. Citizens of the new land were now citizens of the United States. People who had not been citizens—including most native Hawaiians—could not be American citizens.

The Monroe Doctrine was changing the entire world. Other islands in the Pacific Ocean were also being changed. Like Hawaii, these islands also had their own stories to tell.

Map of Cuba from 1616

Chapter Three
CUBA

More than 500 years ago, a man named Hatuey led a group of canoes to an island in the Atlantic Ocean. When he landed, he told a story to the islanders who lived there. His story made them tremble with fear.

Hatuey said white-skinned men had come to his land. They had been dressed in shiny metal. They carried weapons harder than stone. They were cruel. They treated human beings worse than they treated animals. They had killed and hurt Hatuey's people. The only thing they cared about was gold.

These white-skinned men would come to this island too, Hatuey warned. He wanted the islanders to help him fight the strangers.

The islanders couldn't believe Hatuey's story. Only a few of them agreed to help him fight the light-skinned men.

DID YOU KNOW?

Cuba is the largest island in a group of islands that makes up the modern-day Republic of Cuba. Cuba is about ninety miles (about 150 kilometers) south of Florida. It is a little smaller than the state of Pennsylvania.

BEYOND OUR SHORES: AMERICA EXTENDS ITS REACH

Hatuey was right, though. The strangers came to the island. Hatuey and his followers tried to fight them. They lost. They were killed.

Hatuey was Cuba's first hero. His story was changed forever in 1492 when people from Europe first came to the Western Hemisphere.

SPAIN AND CUBA

Spain was disappointed that they didn't find more gold than they did on islands like Cuba. But the Spanish soon realized they could get rich from Cuba in other ways.

THE HEMISPHERES

If we looked at our planet from outer space, it would look like a huge blue ball. If we cut the ball in half from top to bottom, we would have hemispheres. "Hemi" means half, and a sphere is round—so a hemisphere is half of something round. The Earth's Eastern Hemisphere has Africa, Australia, Europe, and Asia. People who come from this part of the world sometimes call it the "Old World." The Western Hemisphere has what today we call the "Americas." Once they found out it was there, people in the Eastern Hemisphere called the Western Hemisphere the "New World." But it wasn't new to the millions of people who had lived there for thousands of years!

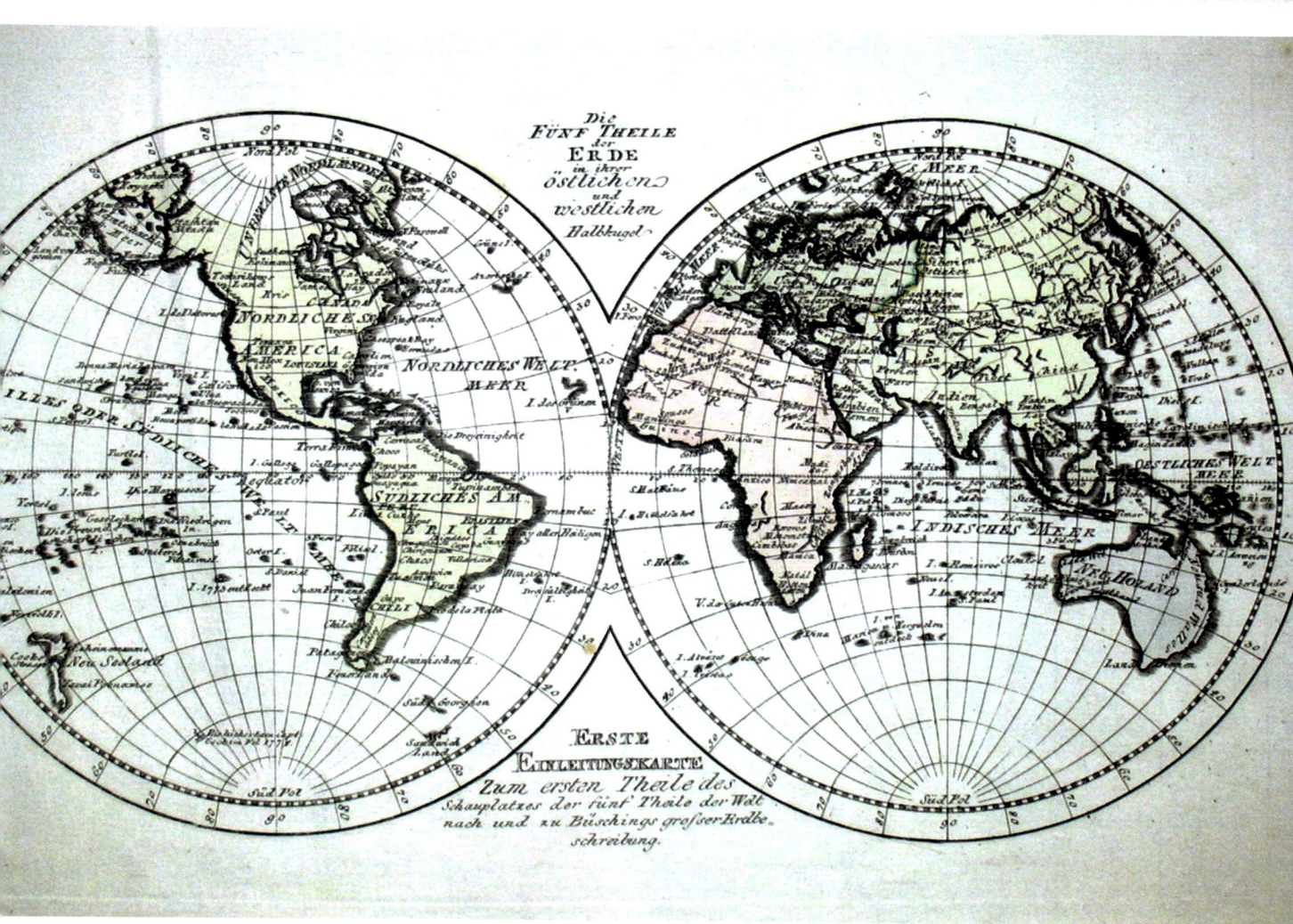

Map of the Earth's hemispheres from 1791.

BEYOND OUR SHORES: AMERICA EXTENDS ITS REACH

Columbus being greeted by Arawak Indians upon his landing.

CHRISTOPHER COLUMBUS AND THE ARAWAKS

In 1492, when Columbus landed in the Western Hemisphere, he believed he had traveled full circle around the world. He thought he had landed in the Indies, a part of Asia. That's why he called the people he met "Indians." Really, however, he had landed in the Bahamas in the Caribbean Sea.

Columbus explored the Bahamas and some of the other islands. Then he went home. He brought stories with him. These were powerful stories. They told about a land filled with gold and riches. They told of people who would make perfect slaves.

Columbus came back to the islands. Many other Spaniards followed. They found peaceful native people called the Arawaks. There were hundreds of thousands of them, maybe even millions. They gave food and friendship to the newcomers. The Spaniards made them into slaves. They killed them. Without meaning to, they also spread new germs to them. In just two years, hundreds of thousands of Arawaks died. Within 50 years, only a few hundred of them were left. In 150 years, every single Arawak was probably dead.

BEYOND OUR SHORES: AMERICA EXTENDS ITS REACH

The island had good farmland. And it turned out sugarcane grew well there. Sugarcane became Cuba's new "gold."

The Spanish built huge sugarcane farms called plantations. These plantations needed lots of workers. The native people were all dead, though. So the Spanish brought slaves to Cuba from Africa.

Three hundred years after Columbus came to Cuba, the people who lived there were completely different. The Arawaks were all gone. Instead, Africans and Spaniards lived there. Some of the Africans and Spaniards had had children together—and then these children had had children of their own.

These groups of people wanted different things. Some of them wanted to be completely free from Spain. They wanted to be their own country.

The landing of the Spanish in Cuba.

CUBA

A MAN WHO WOULD BE PRESIDENT

One of the soldiers who fought in the Spanish-American War was man named Teddy Roosevelt. He led a troop called the Rough Riders. Roosevelt and the Rough Riders helped win the war. Many Americans thought of Roosevelt as a hero.

One day he would become the President of the United States!

Teddy Roosevelt and the other Rough Riders.

BEYOND OUR SHORES: AMERICA EXTENDS ITS REACH

Others wanted to stay a part of Spain. And still others wanted to become part of the United States. By the early 1890s, all these groups of people had been fighting against each other and against Spain for more than 20 years. They were worn out. Their country was poor.

But they didn't give up. In 1895, yet another rebellion began. Spain hit back. Hard. But the Cuban rebels didn't give up. People kept fighting for three more years. And now Americans were getting interested.

The U.S. government kept a close eye on the revolution. There were American businesses in Cuba. Thousands of American citizens lived in Cuba. The United States wanted to protect these people and businesses.

The United States was also interested in making Cuba a state. It wanted Cuba for some of the same reasons that Spain had. Cuba had good land. It could make the United States a lot of money.

For a while, the United States didn't do any fighting in Cuba. They did send some battleships to wait off the coast. One day, a ship named the U.S.S. *Maine* mysteriously exploded. We still don't know why. But Americans were sure that Spain had done it.

The United States went to war against Spain. Suddenly, the Cuban revolution changed names. It was now the Spanish-American War.

DID YOU KNOW?

Sugarcane, the plant from which most of our sugar comes, was first grown in Asia. Europeans brought it to the Western Hemisphere.

CUBA

THE PHILIPPINES AND GUAM

As a result of the Spanish-American War, the United States got even more land from Spain besides Cuba. The Philippines, a group of islands in the Pacific Ocean, also became U.S. land. So did Guam, another Pacific island.

Four months later, the fighting was over. Spain surrendered. But not to Cuban rebels. It surrendered to the United States.

Now, instead of Spain as their ruler, Cubans had the United States. Cubans had wanted complete freedom. They were free from Spain now. But they were worried about becoming part of the United States.

The American military was in Cuba. The United States took part in making Cuba's new government. It took over Cuban trade. It seemed like the United States was taking over Cuba.

Wreck of the U.S.S *Maine*.

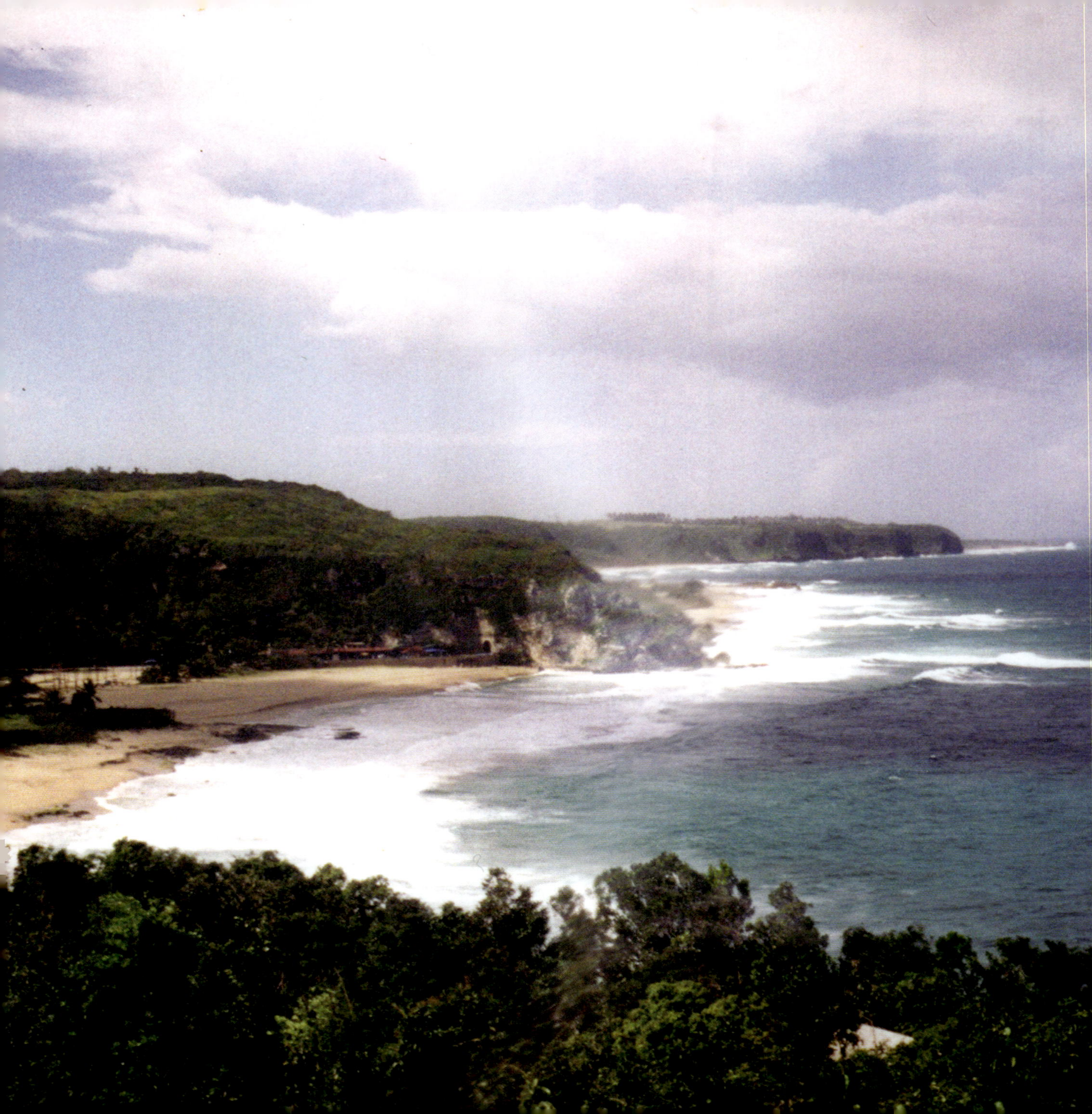

Chapter Four
PUERTO RICO

Some Americans called the Spanish-American War "a splendid little war." They thought it had been an easy war to fight. And in the end, the United States ended up with more land. Cuba was now part of the United States. So were the Philippines. And so was another Caribbean island, Puerto Rico.

THE HISTORY OF PUERTO RICO

A long time ago, there were only a few people who lived on the island of Puerto Rico. These Natives were called the Arawaks. They were short. They had straight, black hair.

WAR

Actually, no war is splendid! Many people were hurt and died in the Spanish-American War. More than 2,000 American soldiers died during the war. And in the Philippines, about 20,000 Filipino soldiers died in the fighting with the United States.

BEYOND OUR SHORES: AMERICA EXTENDS ITS REACH

They wore a lot of jewelry made out of shells, bones, clay, and gold. They didn't wear a lot of clothes.

They didn't call their island Puerto Rico. That's a Spanish name. These people didn't speak Spanish. Instead, they spoke their own language. In their language, the island was called Boriquen.

The Arawaks sometimes fought with another group of people, called the Caribs. They mostly lived in peace, though. That all changed when new people came from Spain.

The Arawaks looked pretty strange to the Columbus and his crew when they first landed back in 1493. The Arawaks had dark skin. They didn't wear many clothes. They spoke a different language. The Spanish looked pretty strange to the Arawaks, too. They had light skin and beards. They had huge wooden ships that rose high out of the water. The men had metal armor and weapons like swords and pistols.

Christopher Columbus

The Spanish renamed everything. They couldn't speak the native language so they named the island and its people in Spanish. They called the Arawaks "Tainos." They called the island's biggest city "Puerto Rico."

Columbus eventually left, but in 1508, a man named Ponce de León came back. He came back to build a fort. He also wanted to colonize the island. That means he brought lots of people to live there. He brought farmers. He brought priests. He brought builders. He brought all the people he needed to make a Spanish town.

Ponce de León claimed the island for Spain. This meant Spain owned it. Ponce de León didn't care about the Arawaks. He didn't ask them if they wanted to give up their island. They had lived there a long time—but now, the Spanish took over.

The Spanish started digging for gold. They wanted to get rich. That was why they wanted the island.

The Arawak

They also made the Arawaks into slaves. They wanted the Arawaks to be more like the Spanish. So they made them wear Spanish clothes. They made them worship God the way the Spanish did. They taught them the Spanish language.

BEYOND OUR SHORES: AMERICA EXTENDS ITS REACH

Some of the Arawaks tried to fight back. But the Spanish were too strong. They killed six thousand Arawaks. By now, most of the native people had disappeared. Some had died. Some had run away to live somewhere else. The island was Spanish.

The Spanish started farming the island. Puerto Rico had good land. It could grow good food. It could also grow sugarcane. Sugarcane is made into sugar. Sugar used to be very expensive. If you could grow and sell sugar, you would be rich.

Who would do the farming? All the native slaves had either died or escaped. The Spanish wouldn't do the farming. They didn't want to do all the hard work. There weren't enough of them either. So they brought in more slaves. This time, they shipped slaves in from Africa. The Africans worked on the sugar farms.

It wasn't an easy life for anyone. People kept on dying of disease. Even the Spanish died. Pirates and Native groups attacked the island. People knew the Spanish were getting rich in Puerto Rico. The Spanish had found gold, silver, and pearls. Thieves attacked the Spanish so they could steal the treasure.

After awhile, the treasure ran out. Even farming wasn't good. Puerto Rico became poor. The Spanish people didn't really want to live there anymore. Most of them moved away.

Spain kept forts on Puerto Rico to protect the land. Armies from other countries kept attacking the forts. They wanted to own the island in the Caribbean, including Puerto Rico.

Who lived on Puerto Rico now? There were two groups of people. One group was Spanish. They had moved to Puerto Rico straight from Spain. Or they were born in Puerto Rico but had two parents who were Spanish. The Spanish people living in Puerto Rico were rich. They owned big farms. They had slaves.

There was another group of people, too. They were called Creoles. When the Spanish first came to Puerto Rico, some of them married Natives. Later, Africans came to the

PUERTO RICO

One of Puerto Rico's Spanish forts.

BEYOND OUR SHORES: AMERICA EXTENDS ITS REACH

island. Some Spanish people married them. The children of parents who came from two different types of people were called Creoles. A Creole person might have an African mother and a Spanish father. Or she could have a Native mother and an African father. Creole just meant that you weren't pure Spanish.

Creoles were poor. They farmed tiny pieces of land. They lived in small huts. People thought Creoles were not as good as the Spanish.

Spain didn't treat Puerto Ricans very well. The **governors** of the island were cruel. They were especially cruel to Africans, Natives, and Creoles. Puerto Rico wanted to be free from Spain.

THE UNITED STATES AND PUERTO RICO

After the Spanish-American War, Puerto Rico belonged to the United States. Now American controlled Puerto Rico. Puerto Ricans were glad to be free from Spain—but they weren't sure yet whether they wanted to be part of the United States.

Now America was building its own empire, just like England had. Americans were proud that their country was growing. Many Americans truly believed that other lands would be better off if they belonged to the United States. They believed that if the United States kept spreading, getting bigger and bigger, the world would be a better place.

And as the country entered the twentieth century, it wasn't just growing larger. It was also growing more powerful. Soon it would be ready to take the lead in one of the biggest wars the world had ever known.

Governors are people who run the government of a town or region.

PUERTO RICO

Political cartoon portraying the "American Empire."

WHAT DO YOU THINK?

Americans told themselves a story that said it would be good for people in other lands to belong to the United States. Do you think there were any other stories being told at the same time? What story do you think the people of Hawaii told their children about the United States' takeover? What story did the people of Cuba, the Philippines, and Puerto Rico tell? Do you think there were more than one story to tell in each of these islands? Do you think just one story was true? Or could more than one story be true?

FIND OUT MORE

In Books

Gutner, Howard. *Puerto Rico.* Chicago: Children's Press, 2009.

Roque, Ismael. *Cuba for Kids.* London, UK: Cuba for Kids Foundation, 2000.

Schraff, Anne. *A Ticket to Philippines.* Minneapolis, Minn.: Carolrhoda, 2001.

Stanley, Faye. *The Last Princess: The Story of Princess Ka'iulani of Hawaii.* New York: HarperCollins, 2001.

On the Internet

Cuba
www.historyofcuba.com
www.nationsonline.org/oneworld/History/Cuba-history.htm

Hawaii
www.gohawaii.com/
www.lava,net/~poda/history.html

Philippines
www.philippine-history.org
www.philippines.hvu.nl

Puerto Rico
Welcome.topuertorico.org
www.smithsonianmag.com/travel/destination-hunter/north-america/caribbean-atlantic/puerto-rico/puerto-rico-history-heritage.html

Spanish-American War
www.loc.gov/rr/hispanic/1898

Teddy Roosevelt and the Rough Riders
www.theodoreroosevelt.org/life/rough_riders.htm

INDEX

Arawak 30–32, 37–40

Christianity 21
Cleveland, Grover 10, 13
Columbus, Christopher 30–32, 38, 39
Cook, James 21, 22
Creoles 40, 42
Cuba 27–35

Dole, James Drummond 22, 23, 25

Hatuey 27, 28
Hawaii 17–25
Hawaiian Pineapple Company 22, 23
hemisphere 28–31

international tribunal 13
irrigation 18

Monroe Doctrine 10, 13, 15, 22, 25
Monroe, James 10, 15

plantations 32
Polynesia 18
Princess Kaiulani 24, 25
Puerto Rico 37–43

Revolutionary War 9
Roosevelt, Teddy 33, 45

slave 31, 32, 39, 40

ABOUT THE AUTHOR

Constance Sharp studied history and literature in college. She enjoys teaching children about the history of their world.

ABOUT THE CONSULTANT

Dr. Jack N. Rakove is a professor of history and American studies at Stanford University, where he is director of American studies. The winner of the 1997 Pulitzer Prize in history, Dr. Rakove is the author of *The Unfinished Election of 2000, Constitutional Culture and Democratic Rule*, and *James Madison and the Creation of the American Republic*. He is also the president of the Society for the History of the Early American Republic.

PICTURE CREDITS
Benjamin Stewart: p. 33, 43
British National Archives: p. 11
Charles Johnson Post: p. 33
Franz Johann Joseph von Reilly: p. 29
Hawaiian State Archives: p. 22, 24
Hemera Image: p. 14, 16
National Archives and Records Administration: p. 35
Photos.com: p. 8

Roxanna Stevens: p. 36, 41
Theodor de Bry: p. 30
William James Hubbard: p. 15

To the best knowledge of the publisher, all other images are in the public domain. If any image has been inadvertently uncredited, please notify Harding House Publishing Services, Vestal, New York 13850, so that rectification can be made for future printings.

48